Clothes /
J 677THO

W9-CMU-239
Solon Public Library

Thomson, Ruth,
Solon Public Library

DATE DUE

NOV 0 6 2012			
DEC 0 8 2012			
FEB 0 8 2014			
MAR 0 9 2015			
APR 2 1 2015			

DEMCO 128-5046

Solon Public Library
320 W. Main
Solon, IA 52333

recycling & reusing

Clothes

Ruth Thomson

Photography by Neil Thomson

A+
Smart Apple Media

First published in 2006 by Franklin Watts
338 Euston Road, London NW1 3BH

Franklin Watts Australia, Hachette Children's Books
Level 17/207 Kent Street, Sydney NSW 2000

This edition published under license from Franklin Watts. All rights reserved.
Copyright © 2006 Franklin Watts

Editor: Rachel Cooke, Design: Holly Mann,
Art Director: Rachel Hamdi, Consultant: Michelle Barry, LMB London

Text copyright © Ruth Thomson 2006
Photographs copyright © Neil Thomson 2006

Additional photography
Franklin Watts 6, 7, 11b, 15b, 21tr; Picanol 9c; LMB London 10r, 12; Recycle now 10bl, 11t, 26t;
Lucy Bateman and Etienne Oliff 27tr and c; Jenny Matthews 12 and 26br

Published in the United States by Smart Apple Media
2140 Howard Drive West, North Mankato, Minnesota 56003

U.S. publication copyright © 2007 Smart Apple Media
International copyright reserved in all countries. No part
of this book may be reproduced in any form without
written permission from the publisher.
Printed in the United States of America

Library of Congress Cataloging-in-Publication Data

Thomson, Ruth, 1949-
Clothes / by Ruth Thomson.
p. cm. — (Recycling and reusing)
Includes index.
ISBN-13: 978-1-58340-939-8
1. Textile fabrics—Juvenile literature. 2. Recycling
(Waste, etc.)—Juvenile literature. [1. Clothing and
dress—Juvenile literature.] I. Title.

TT497.T46 2006
677.0028'6—dc22   2006000020

9 8 7 6 5 4 3 2 1

Contents

Words printed in **bold** are explained in the glossary

What are clothes like?

How would you live without clothes? They keep you warm in cold weather and dry in wet weather. They protect your skin from the wind and hot sun and keep you comfortable at night.

Cotton clothes are fine and smooth. Cotton lets your skin breathe. It soaks up sweat and keeps you cool in hot weather.

T-shirts are made of knitted cotton.

Jeans are made of a tough kind of cotton **fabric** called denim.

Wool clothes are soft and springy.

Wool traps air between its **fibers** and keeps you warm in cold weather.

Some clothes are made of **synthetic** fabrics.
These are usually very strong.

Some synthetic
fabrics are
waterproof.

IT'S A FACT

Nylon, polyester, viscose, and acrylic are synthetic fabrics. Some fabrics are made of a mixture of synthetics.

Some synthetic
fabrics are stretchy.

Look at the labels on your clothes to find out what they are made from.

Clothes are washable.
When clothes get dirty, they can be washed
in soap and water to make them
clean again.

Rip!
If you catch your clothes on
something sharp, they will tear.

Making textiles

Textiles for clothes are made from long, thin, bendable threads known as fibers.

Fine fibers

Natural fibers come from animals, plants, or insects. Synthetic fibers are made in factories from oil, coal, and wood.

Wool from a sheep is dirty and greasy.

Cleaned wool is spun and **dyed**.

Acrylic fibers are made from oil.

Wool fibers come from the coats of sheep, goats, or rabbits.

Spinning

The fibers must be stretched and twisted so that they overlap to make long threads called **yarn**. This is called spinning.

Cotton fibers come from the seedpod of the cotton plant.

Silk fibers come from the cocoons that silkworms spin.

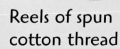

Reels of spun cotton thread

Warp yarns

Weft yarn

Weaving

Most yarn is woven on a **loom**. A loom holds taut lengthwise threads, spaced closely side by side. These are called the warp yarns. Another thread, called the weft yarn, criss-crosses the warp yarns from one side to the other.

Factory looms

Huge automatic looms weave cloth in **factories**. Blasts of air or metal arms move the weft yarn back and forth.

Knitting

Yarn can also be knitted. Knitting uses one long yarn that is looped and knotted together in rows.

LOOK AND SEE

Try stretching a pair of jeans and a knitted scarf. The scarf is stretchier. The knitted loops become wider as you pull. Denim jeans are tightly woven. The threads cannot stretch very far.

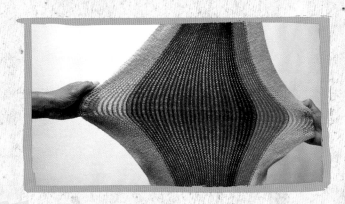

Giving away clothes

It is a waste to throw away clothes that you have out-grown or no longer want.

Filling up landfill

If you put clothes with your garbage, they will just be buried at a **landfill site** and take up valuable space.

Clothing banks

Put clean, unwanted clothes into a clothing bank. You could also give them to a charity.

IT'S A FACT

Almost three-quarters of the garments put in clothing banks are sold as secondhand clothes.

Sorted by hand

The clothes go to a huge warehouse. Here, people carefully sort them by type, size, and material.

Charity stores

When people buy secondhand clothes in charity stores, they help raise money for good causes.

YOU CAN HELP

- *Pass on clothes that no longer fit to smaller friends, brothers, or sisters.*
- *Put unwanted clothes in plastic bags to keep them clean and dry for taking to a clothing bank.*
- *Cut up old cotton clothes to use as cleaning rags.*
- *Use old clothes for messy activities.*

Reused or recycled

Good clothes can be worn again.
Unwearable clothes are cut or shredded.

Secondhand sales

Many secondhand clothes are resold to Africa, Asia, and Eastern Europe. Stores and traders sell the clothes cheaply to people who could not afford more expensive new clothes.

Nothing wasted

Very worn T-shirts, sweatshirts, and cotton pants are cut up and turned into wiping cloths for all types of cleaning.

Buttons and zippers are cut off clothes used as wiping cloths.

Shredded into shoddy

Completely unusable clothes are **recycled**. They are torn into fibers that are known as **shoddy**. To make shoddy, these **sanitation workers** in Egypt feed clothes by hand into a machine.

Shoddy

The clothes go in one end. . .

. . . and come out the other end as shoddy.

Padding and filling

This delivery man in Morocco is bringing shoddy to a furniture workshop. It will be used as mattress filling or chair and sofa padding. Shoddy is also used as sound **insulation** material.

Crafty clothes

Some fashion designers create new garments by combining pieces of secondhand clothes.

A unique vest

The vest below is made from several printed silk scarves. They were sewn together and cut into shape.

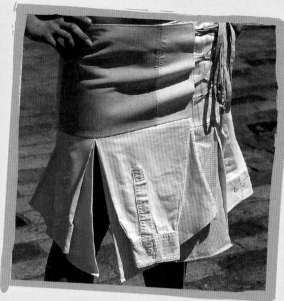

Detail of the vest pockets

A shirt skirt

Can you see the sleeves of an old shirt that make up part of this skirt?

An unusual belt

This belt is made with men's ties. The cut ends have been sewn onto the waistband of an old pair of jeans.

Hand-crafted hats

Some designers recycle unusual materials into new hats.

Tough tarpaulin

Some Brazilian designers make caps and hats, as well as bags and jackets, from old **tarpaulin**.

A hat made from the front of a woolly cardigan

A summer hat woven from rolled paper

A tarpaulin cap

A cowboy hat made from pieces of old jeans

YOUR TURN

Give new life to a T-shirt or an old pair of jeans.

- *Paint or print a design onto the T-shirt.*
- *Cut off the legs of the jeans to turn them into shorts.*

Cutting up clothes

People also cut up old clothes and use the pieces to make something completely different.

A patterned prayer rug

A rugmaker used cloth **snippets** for this rug. Notice how she carefully arranged the snippets by color to make patterns.

A striped mat

This floor mat was woven with long strips cut from old clothes.

A smart saddle blanket

Clothes scraps were poked through a piece of **burlap** to make the saddle blanket on this donkey.

A patchwork folder

The cover of this folder is made from scraps of fabric sewn together.

A sock puppet

Don't throw away odd or worn socks. Make funny puppets with them.

Sew on buttons for the eyes, nose, and mouth.

A pretty photo album

Sparkly cloth scraps decorate the front of this photo album.

Waste not, want not

When factories cut out clothes, there are always fabric scraps left over.

Scrap originals

Girls at a school for sanitation workers in Cairo learn how to weave rugs and bags with scraps.

1. They learn to sort the scraps by color and material.

2. This girl is weaving scraps on a loom. She leaves the ends loose.

3. She takes the finished fabric off the loom and trims it. Then she sews up the sides to make a bag.

The handles are made of braided scraps.

Patchwork pieces

Egyptian craftswomen make **quilts** or pillows with scraps. They cut out pieces of fabric that will fit together, using cardboard shapes as a guide. These shapes are called templates.

Cardboard template

Comfy cushions

They sew the pieces together to make cushion covers.

Saving scraps

In countries where cloth is expensive, people save every spare scrap.

Teeny bikinis

This dressmaker in Brazil uses tiny pieces of cloth left over from making tops to make bikinis.

Stylish scrunchies

Some people make hair scrunchies like these by threading elastic through fabric scraps.

Rag dolls

People often make rag dolls for children from cloth scraps.

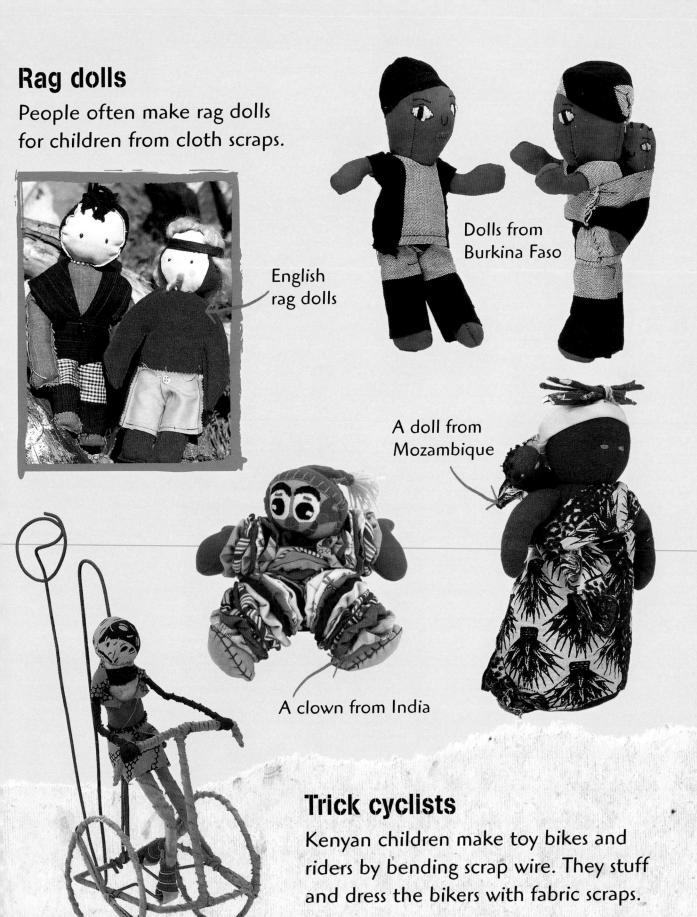

English rag dolls

Dolls from Burkina Faso

A doll from Mozambique

A clown from India

Trick cyclists

Kenyan children make toy bikes and riders by bending scrap wire. They stuff and dress the bikers with fabric scraps.

21

T-shirt strips

When factories make T-shirt fabric, there are long strips left over. Craftworkers use them to make all sorts of things.

Balls of T-shirt fabric strips

A woven wall hanging

1. This weaver has tied lengths of string from top to bottom on a wooden frame. She weaves the fabric strips between the strings.

3. She pushes the strips down into place with a toothed tool.

2. She weaves different colors to build up a picture.

Each weaver chooses a different picture or pattern to make.

Brand-new bags

The fabric strips are also used to make handbags.

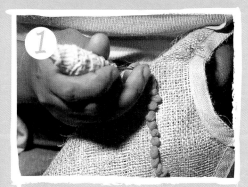

1. The maker pushes the strips through a shaped piece of burlap.

2. She builds up a pattern, which covers the burlap.

3. She sews up the sides of the burlap and adds a zipper to finish the bag.

Finished bags on sale

Cotton paper

In India, people recycle cuttings from white cotton T-shirts and work gloves to make handmade paper.

Paper with strands of **algae**

Paper with sugar cane fibers

Paper with wool fibers

Paper with marigold petals

Paper with recycled **jute** sacks

Making paper

The cotton is shredded into tiny pieces, soaked, and beaten into **pulp** by a machine. Sometimes dye is added to color the paper.

1. The pulp is poured onto a **mold and deckle**, which sit in a vat of water.

3. The paper is tipped onto a piece of **felt**. This soaks up some more of the water.

4. The paper is stacked with other sheets in a press, which squeezes out more water. Finally, the sheets are separated and hung up to dry.

2. When they are lifted out, water drains away, leaving a sheet of very wet paper on the **mesh** of the mold.

Patterned paper

Cotton paper is made into sketch books, photo frames, notebooks, and photograph albums.

IT'S A FACT

Dollar bills are made of cotton paper because it is so strong and durable.

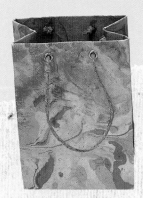

Paper bags

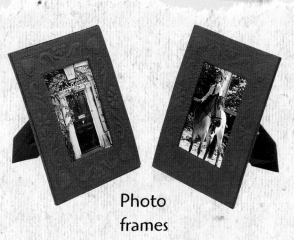

Photo frames

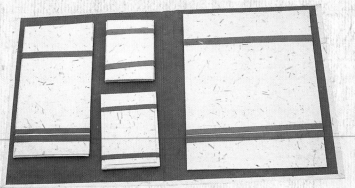

Writing paper

Notebooks

Writing paper and envelopes speckled with old dollar bills

25

Saving shoes

Do you throw away your unwanted or outgrown shoes when you buy new ones? Most discarded shoes are reusable.

IT'S A FACT

Some companies are recycling shoes to create new basketball courts, tennis courts, and running tracks.

Resoled and resold

Put unwanted shoes and sandals into a shoe or clothing bank. Some pairs of shoes are sold in charity stores. Many more are sent to countries where new shoes are expensive.

Cobblers make the shoes as good as new. Traders resell them at prices local people can afford.

YOU CAN HELP

When you give away unwanted shoes, remember to join them in pairs, either with an elastic band or by tying the laces together

Flip-flop-a-lu-la

Hundreds of old flip-flops wash onto the beach of a marine nature reserve in Kenya. Local women collect them as they gather firewood. This helps keep the beach clean, and the women make money by turning the flip-flops into toys and jewelry.

They cut up the flip-flops, shaping them into bath toys and key rings.

Jazzy jewelry

Some of the women string small pieces of flip-flops together into bracelets and necklaces. They add shells as extra decoration.

Bracelet

Necklace

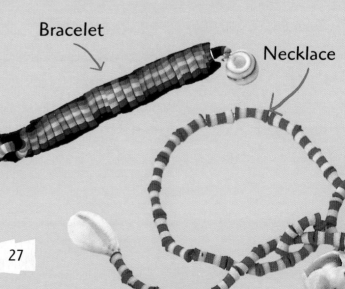

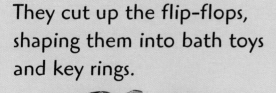

Flip-flop key rings

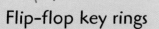

Glossary

algae a type of plant, such as seaweed

burlap a strong fabric made from the jute plant

dyed given a new color

fabric cloth

factory a building where things are made in large numbers using machines

felt a sheet of thick, matted wool

fiber a thin strand that comes from a plant or an animal, or is made artificially from oil, coal, or wood pulp

insulation a covering that stops something, such as heat, electricity, or sound, from passing through it

jute a tall plant with strong, stringy fibers used to make bags, ropes, sacks, and carpet backs

landfill site a huge pit in the ground where crushed garbage is buried

loom equipment for weaving fabric

mesh criss-crossed wires with tiny holes between them

mold and deckle handmade paper-making equipment. The mold is a frame with wire mesh stretched over it. The deckle is a frame with edges that hold the pulp in place

pulp a mass of soft, broken-down fibers mixed with water for paper-making

recycle to use an existing object or material to make something new

sanitation worker someone who makes a living collecting and sorting garbage

shoddy the torn-up fibers of old clothes

snippet a little piece of fabric cut with scissors

synthetic made by people or machines, not by nature

tarpaulin tough, waterproof material spread over goods in an open truck or boat to keep them from getting wet

textile a woven or knitted fabric

waterproof not letting water in or out

yarn spun thread

Guess what?

- Clothes and other textiles, such as sheets, curtains, and blankets, make up between three and five percent of household garbage.

- More than 70 percent of the world uses secondhand clothes. Almost any clothes you don't want anymore—including swimwear, sneakers, football cleats, caps, snow suits, pajamas, and even socks —will be useful to someone somewhere.

- Synthetic clothes do not rot in landfill sites, so it is better to pass them on than to throw them away.

- Today, many clothes are thrown away because they have gone out of fashion, not because they are worn-out, outgrown, or torn.

Useful Web sites

http://www.epa.gov/recyclecity/
See how Dumptown became Recycle City with fun games and interesting facts about recycling clothes and other materials

http://www.nike.com/nikebiz/nikego/
Learn about the Nike Reuse-A-Shoe program and how old shoes can be recycled to make basketball courts, running tracks, and more

http://www.olliesworld.com/planet/usa/index.htm
Ollie's World is a fun, interactive Web site that includes information and tips about reusing and recycling

http://www.planetpals.com/earthday.html
Projects and information about Earth Day, America Recycles Day, and other events that promote recycling

Index